The **Essential** Buyer's Guide

DUCATI

DESMODUE

Pantah, F1, 750 Sport, 600, 750 900 1000
Supersport, ST2, Monster, SportClassic 1979 to 2013

T0386360

VELOCE PUBLISHING
THE PUBLISHER OF FINE AUTOMOTIVE BOOKS

www.veloce.co.uk

For post publication news, updates and amendments relating to this book please visit www.veloce.co.uk/books/V4567

First published in March 2014 by Veloce Publishing Limited, Veloce House, Parkway Farm Business Park, Middle Farm Way, Poundbury, Dorchester, Dorset, DT1 3AR, England.
Fax 01305 250479/e-mail info@veloce.co.uk/web www.veloce.co.uk or www.velocebooks.com.

ISBN: 978-1-845845-67-4 UPC: 6-36847-04567-8

Ubiquitous and enduring is how the range of Ducati belt-driven two-valve motorcycles can be described. In the mid-1970s, Ducati's great engineer Fabio Taglioni originally conceived the two-valve belt-driven twins, or Desmodue, as mid-displacement models to replace the unloved parallel twin. Little did he realise that this same basic engine design that began life as a 500 prototype in 1976 would grow to 1100cc, and still be powering Ducatis nearly 40 years later. Furthermore, the basic crankcase design influenced all Ducati twins until the advent of the Panigale in 2012.

The impetus for the creation of the belt-drive two-valve engine was economics. By the mid-1970s, Ducati's traditional bevel-drive overhead camshaft singles and twins were simply becoming uneconomic to produce, and Taglioni saw the toothed belt camshaft drive as the solution. In the process he incorporated a forged one-piece crankshaft, and immediately solved most of the reliability

The first Desmodue was the 500 Pantah. This is a 1981 version.

problems that afflicted the bevel-drive twins. The belt-drive Pantah went on to win four successive World TT2 titles in the hands of Tony Rutter before forming the basis for the next generation of Ducati engines, the all-conquering Desmoquattro. With the release of the Desmoquattro Superbike as the range leader, the simpler two-valve engine was relegated to an alternative role. It initially powered the Paso and Supersport, then the Monster and Sport Touring, and more recently the Hypermotard and SportClassic. Along the way there were several parallel line-ups, notably the Cagiva Elefant and Gran Canyon.

The two-valve belt-drive twins have always appealed to a different clientele than the more complex Desmoquattro and Testastretta. Although they produce considerably less power, these engines are easier to live with, and servicing is considerably simpler and less expensive. They also continue the Ducati tradition of achieving more through less, with an emphasis on performance through a balance of power and weight. Unlike the Superbikes, they are not intimidating to ride or own.

This book is intended to be a straightforward guide to the belt-drive Desmodue, an engine that has been Ducati's mainstay for nearly 40 years. Before the Desmodue, Ducatis were considered idiosyncratic and eccentric, with questionable long-term reliability. Although it still drew heavily on earlier designs, the Pantah rewrote Ducati's DNA. In addition, since Ducati's manufacturing plant was updated many thousands more of these new motorcycles have been produced than in earlier decades. Ducatis went from being limited edition, unobtainable motorcycles, to being much more readily available. As a result, the market is awash with used examples.

Today, a Desmodue makes an excellent second-hand buy. Only the rare 750 F1 limited edition series and the MH 900E have earned classic status, and, as the regular production versions

Monsters have been a mainstay of the Desmodue line-up for twenty years. This is the S2R of 2005.

The gradual expansion of the Desmodue range saw the popular Hypermotard released for 2007.

were sold in relatively large numbers, there's a wide choice available at surprisingly low prices. When you buy a Desmodue you are also buying into a legend. Covered here are the Pantah and later Desmodue models, in capacities from 350 through 1100cc.

The Essential Buyer's Guide™ currency
At the time of publication a BG unit of currency "●" equals approximately £1.00/US$1.62/Euro 1.20. Please adjust to suit current exchange rates using Sterling (£) as the base currency.

Contents

1 Is it the right bike for you?

– marriage guidance

Tall and short riders

Generally, Italian bikes are designed for Italians, and thus suit shorter riders. The Supersport family from 1989-1998 has one of the most comfortable sporting riding positions. The post-1998 Supersport and SportClassic have a more aggressive riding position, with low bars and relatively high footpegs. Anyone over six foot may find these sporting bikes quite uncomfortable, and even the Monsters suffer from a low seat and high pegs. The ST2 and ST3, SportClassic 1000 GT, 907 (ie Paso, Hypermotard and Multistrada) are the most suitable for taller riders.

Running costs

These are much more economical bikes to own than the more complex Desmoquattro series. Servicing is not as time-consuming, and they are not as heavy on tyres, chains, and brakes. New spares are expensive, but there's a good choice of second-hand spares available. Fuel consumption is around 40-45mpg, with the smaller capacities the most economical.

Maintenance

Although all Ducatis are relatively high maintenance bikes, requiring careful upkeep, the simpler two-valve, air-cooled range is the easiest to live with. This applies in particular to the carburettor-equipped versions, in that they're more reminiscent of an earlier era. Service intervals have gradually increased over the years, but are generally at 6000 mile intervals, with oil changes at 3000 miles. Valve adjustment and timing belt replacement is far less time-consuming than on a Desmoquattro, so the cost of servicing is a lot less.

Usability

The appeal of the two-valve motor is its everyday usability and easy-going performance. While the Desmoquattro makes around 30-40 per cent more power for a similar displacement, these engines run very hot and can be unpleasant in warmer climates or heavy traffic. As it generates a lot less heat, the Desmodue is more suited to these situations (the Desmodue Monster being ideal for everyday use).

Parts availability

Excellent, except for the earliest Pantahs and F1s that are now around thirty years old. A lot of engine parts carried through over the years, and there's a good selection of aftermarket or second-hand bodywork spares available from breakers.

Parts costs

Service parts are reasonable, but other parts are expensive, especially bodywork and exhaust systems. Working second-hand parts with some sort of warranty are a good, cheaper alternative.

Insurance group

Ducati Desmodues generally fall into lower insurance groups than the more sporting Ducatis. The Monster 696 is in Group 11, while even the SportClassic 1000 S is only Group 15. The model with the highest insurance category is the Hypermotard, at Group 17.

Investment potential
Due to the large number of bikes built, investment potential is limited. Only the limited edition F1 series is likely to become really collectable, although any well-preserved older model should increase in value. Some of the SportClassic and MH 900Es have already become collectors' items, but less likely investment prospects are most Monsters, Pasos, STs, Multistradas and Hypermotards. As with all Ducatis, the more sporting models have historically been more collectable, and this will also apply to the Desmodue.

Foibles
Surprisingly few if the maintenance schedule is adhered to. Electrical problems are not uncommon, especially if the battery has gone flat at some stage, but, generally speaking, these bikes are very reliable.

Plus points
The Ducati Desmodue is one of the great motorcycle engines – smooth, torquey, and reliable. Because the engine design has been in production for more than thirty years all the bugs have been ironed out and they are easy to live with.

Minus points
Very few, really, as long as the maintenance schedule has been adhered to. Even a relatively ancient Pantah can make a good everyday motorcycle, and the newer examples are brilliant. Ignoring oil changes is asking for trouble, though, and cam belts must be changed every two years.

Alternatives
Lots of these. Every Japanese and European motorcycle manufacturer has something to take on the Ducati Desmodue. Aprilia has certainly targeted the Monster, and several alternatives to the Hypermotard are available. Ultimately, though, you will buy one of these bikes because it's a Ducati.

One of the rarest and most collectable two-valve Ducatis is the 1986 750 Montjuich.

2 Cost considerations
– affordable, or a money pit?

Compared to the more complexDesmoquattro models, all the two-valve Ducatis will be cheaper to run and maintain. As they don't produce as much power, they are considerably easier on brakes, tyres and chains, and servicing the simpler two-valve desmodromic system is significantly less expensive. From model year 2007, Ducati lengthened service intervals considerably, extending major service intervals from 6000 miles to 7500 miles. Cam belts are required to be changed every two years, and the front forks should be rebuilt every 12,000 miles.

Spares prices
1991-97 900 Supersport (serviceable second-hand parts)
Fairing panel ●x35
Carburettor set ●x200
Instrument set ●x125
Forks (new stanchions/seals) ●x250
Front wheel ●x150
Front brake disc ●x80
Exhaust silencer ●x120
Rear shock ●x150 (recon-250)
ECU unit ●x180

2012 Hypermotard 1100 (new parts)
Air filter ●x15
Battery ●x100
Brake lever ●x25
Brake pads ●x40
Cam timing belt ●x18
Clutch basket ●x150
Clutch lever ●x35 (genuine)
Clutch lever ●x8 (pattern)
Clutch plate set ●x150
ECU ●x200
Exhaust silencer ●x500 (standard pair)
Fork seals ●x40
Fork stanchion ●x300
Front and rear tyre ●x300
Front brake disc ●x175
Front sprocket ●x15
Fuel pump ●x120
Oil filter ●x12
Rear shock ●x1000 (Öhlins)
Rear sprocket ●x25
Rocker cover gasket ●x2.50
Throttle position sensor ●x100
Valve rocker arm ●x30

Wheel bearings ●x8 (each)

Servicing
7500 miles ●x190
15,000 miles ●x250

Tyre wear isn't a serious problem.

Timing belt replacement is neither expensive nor difficult. These are aftermarket timing belt covers.

Brake discs and pads on early 1990s Supersports are not expensive to replace.

3 Living with a Desmodue

– will you get along together?

Ducatis have a reputation for being expensive, demanding and finicky, but two-valve, belt-drive Ducatis are generally easy to live with. They aren't demanding to ride, are reasonably simple to service, and are surprisingly practical as day-to-day transport. Many Desmodues won't cost much to buy, and will happily run all year round, clocking up high mileages.

Spanning this complete range of bikes – sports bike, sports tourer, and naked Monster – is Ducati's venerable Pantah 90-degree V-twin engine. Although it began life as a 500cc in 1979, and has grown to 1100cc over the next 35 years, it remains one of Ducati's finest and most reliable engines. The smaller capacity versions may lack low down torque, but the larger capacity examples provide extremely torquey and relaxed riding. The 90-degree V-twin provides perfect primary balance, so even in 1000 and 1100cc form the engine is remarkably smooth. Because most versions are air or air/oil-cooled, many of these bikes are not physically large or intimidating for shorter riders (no radiators or plumbing means the engine is more compact).

When it comes to the riding position, even the ubiquitous Supersport, until 1998 at least, offered a less extreme sporting set-up than comparable Desmoquattros. And the Multistrada, Hypermotard, Sport Touring, and to a lesser extent the Monster, provide a comfortable riding position, eminently suitable for long-distance riding. These bikes are reasonable alternatives to Japanese and other European offerings for all-round use.

The older Pantahs have 'loose' handling by Ducati standards, and the 750 F1 and Paso were afflicted with a 16-inch front wheel, but all these bikes handle well enough, as you would expect. The Hypermotard is a particularly brilliant B-road scratcher, especially the high-end EVO versions with Öhlins suspension. One major advantage all the two-valve belt-driven bikes have is they are compact and not overly heavy. As a result, even the base models, with basic suspension and brakes, still handle surprisingly well. They are not particularly powerful (in terms of horsepower), and with moderate weight the suspension and brakes are not taxed severely. A Desmodue doesn't really produce enough power to be a formidable track day machine, their forte is as a street bike, and here they are virtually without equal in my opinion. Many people go out and buy a sophisticated, complicated and expensive Desmoquattro when a well-sorted Desmodue would more than suffice for their needs.

Compared to the four-valve models, maintenance of a two-valve Ducati is nowhere near as onerous. But no Ducati is a 'ride and forget it' motorcycle. The desmodromic valve system must be checked reasonably regularly for optimum performance, and the timing belts changed at appropriate intervals. Engine oil should be changed annually, regardless of mileage. Because of the reasonable weight and power these motorcycles are moderately economical on fuel, and not too hard on tyres and chains.

The larger capacity twins, especially fuel-injected types, are tough on batteries and starting systems. If the battery is allowed to run flat, for example, all sorts of electrical problems can appear. The clutch has always been an Achilles heel for large capacity Ducati twins, although this was improved considerably on later examples. These machines don't respond well to neglect, and even when looked after can cause problems. Infrequent use can lead to timing belt failure, injection nozzle rusting, and/or starter clutch and clutch slave cylinder problems.

Unlike the more complex four-valve series, not only routine servicing (oil/filter changes, brake pads and chains), but valve adjustment and even timing belt replacement are well within the capabilities of a competent home mechanic. With a workshop manual, even timing belt replacement is relatively straightforward.

High mileages are not necessarily a problem if the maintenance schedule is adhered to. Often, a regularly well-maintained machine is preferable to one that has been sitting for long periods unused. The timing belts don't respond well to being left in one position for a long time.

Assuming the maintenance isn't a burden, will the riding experience match the hype? The good news is that it will. Get these bikes out into the environment for which they were designed (fast curving roads), and they can still hold their own. Desmodue Ducatis have been around long enough now for a huge fund of knowledge to have built up, and there are plenty of owners clubs and web forums (see the back of this book for details) out there with fellow owners willing to help out.

There's something else that makes the two-valve belt-drive Ducatis particularly appealing. As they have been produced in reasonably large numbers over a long period of time, there is a wide range of bikes available at a reasonable price. For moderate outlay you can buy into the Ducati legend. Ducatis are real riders' bikes: Desmodues are the most affordable, and are fantastic to ride!

Don't be put off by a high mileage.

1990s 900 Supersports represent extremely good value for money, and are reliable and easy to live with.

These bikes aren't particularly heavy on consumables like chains and sprockets.

4 Relative values

– which model for you?

This chapter shows the values, in percentage terms, of individual models in good condition relative to the most affordable: the 600 Monster, 500 SL Pantah and 750 Paso. Desmodue evolution divides into six types, with only the basic engine design shared. The Pantah series was built from 1979 until 1988; the next generation 900 from 1989 until 1998. The fuel-injected 900 arrived in 1998, lasting until 2002. The twin-spark 1000 replaced the 900 in 2003, and later that year came the Desmotre ST3, which can also be considered in this family. The final Desmodue was the 1100 that first appeared in the Hypermotard of 2007, and continues into 2013.

As there were so many variations of Desmodue twins, this chapter looks at the strengths and weaknesses of each model, so you can decide which is best for you.

Models

1979-1986	500/600/650 SL TL Pantah, Cagiva Alazzurra
1985-1988	400 F3 750 F1, Montjuich, Laguna Seca, Santamonica
1986-1989	750 Paso, 750 Sport
1988-1998	906 Paso, 907 ie, 900 Supersport, 900 Superlight, 900 Monster
1990-2001	350/400/600/750 Monster and Supersport
1998-2002	750, 900 ie Supersport, Sport, 900 Monster, 900 MHe, ST2
2002-2007	620, 800, Supersport, Sport, Monster, Multistrada, S2R
2003-2010	1000 DS Multistrada, Monster, Hypermotard, Supersport, Sport Classic
2004-2007	ST3, ST3S
2006-2013	695, 696, 796 Monster, Hypermotard
2007-2013	1100, 1100S Multistrada, Hypermotard, Monster

350/500/600/650 SL TL Pantah, Cagiva Alazzurra, Indiana, Elefant, Gran Canyon

The Pantah began life as the 500 SL, but soon evolved into 350, 600 and 650 variants. During an era of uncertainty at Ducati, the Cagiva takeover of 1985 resulted in a range of Pantah-based models with Cagiva badges. The Cagiva models are quite rare nowadays, and the Elefant and Gran Canyon continued for several more years (the Gran Canyon until 2000). The Pantah really initiated the modern era for Ducati. The engines were simple and reliable; much more so than the previous bevel-drive generation. Prior to the Cagiva takeover there was little money available for design and development, so all of the Pantahs prior to 1985 were very similar underneath. Even the Cagiva Alazzurra was ostensibly a Pantah with slightly different styling. The Indiana remains an enigma

The Pantah is still an under-appreciated classic.

in Ducati history as an unsuccessful attempt to create a cruiser out of the Pantah.

Despite vastly improved reliability, the Pantah, particularly as a 350 and 500, lacked low-end torque. The uninspired styling has meant they haven't really become sought-after and collectable like some earlier Ducatis. They are, however, still bargain classics.
100%

1985-88 350/400 F3 750 F1 Montjuich, Laguna Seca, Santamonica

The success of Tony Rutter on the TT2 (four successive World Championships), saw the release of the 750 F1 in 1985. This evolved into the improved 1986 750 F1, the delectable Montjuich, and two further limited edition F1 series (Laguna Seca and Santamonica). The 350 and 400 F3 were primarily produced for Japan and Italy. By modern standards all the F1s are comparatively rare and are now becoming collectable, particularly the limited edition versions. The F1 marks the end of the era of Ducati under government control, so they still exhibit signs of inconsistent development. Despite a 16-inch front wheel they also steer quite slowly compared to subsequent Cagiva-inspired models. But they are light and reliable, and appeal to traditionalists.
750 F1 250%
350/400 F3 120%
Montjuich/Laguna Seca/Santamonica 500%

1986-89 750 Paso, 750 Sport

Cagiva's influence was immediate, and was reflected in the release of the

The author testing a pre-production 750 F1 in 1985. The F1 is considered by many to represent the end of an era at Ducati.

The F1 was updated for 1986 with new Cagiva graphics. This example also has Montjuich wheels.

For 1987, Ducati released a small number of Laguna Secas.

A short-lived model of the 1980s was the Nuovo 750 Sport.

controversial 750 Paso in 1986. Although the 750 F1 engine was largely unchanged, the 750 Paso featured a number of significant departures from traditional Ducati practice. These included a full cradle box-section steel frame, with a proper rising rate suspension, and fully enclosed bodywork. The Paso also included 16-inch wheels front and rear, with low profile radial tyres, and a reversed rear cylinder head that allowed for the fitting of a controversial automotive style Weber carburettor. It wasn't a successful formula, though, and shortly afterwards Ducati released a new version of the Ducati Sport, still with the 16-inch wheels and Weber carburettor, but with a more traditional tubular steel frame with cantilever rear suspension. Both these models suffered from carburation and reliability problems and have never been especially popular.
100%

1988-98 906 Paso, 907 ie, 900 Supersport, 900 Superlight, 900 Monster

The next generation Desmodue appeared in 1988, initially as the liquid-cooled 906 Paso. Although the 906 still featured the troublesome Weber carburettor, the redesigned crankcases allowed for more displacement and a six-speed gearbox. But the 906 still had 16-inch wheels (regarded as unfashionable) so the next new model, the 900 Supersport, featured 17-inch wheels. This was Ducati's best attempt yet at resurrecting its sporting prowess, but it still didn't quite hit the mark. However, Ducati did hit the bull's-eye with the 1990 900 Supersport, now with Mikuni carburettors and a more comfortable riding position. This Supersport lasted until 1998, and was one of Ducati's standout models of the 1990s. There were still a few problems, but with better electrics and more consistent build these were great bikes, and still offer exceptional value.

From 1992 Ducati offered limited edition versions of the 900 Supersport – the Superlight in Europe and SP in the USA. The 1992 edition was the most special, with composite Marvic wheels and some carbon-fibre components, but all offered some special parts to elevate them above the usual SS. The last Superlight was the 1998 silver Final Edition.

The 907 ie was another short-lived attempt to salvage the Paso concept. Lasting only two years (1991 and 1992), the 907 ie included liquid cooling, Marelli electronic fuel-injection, and 17-inch wheels. Although providing decent performance in a comfortable sport-touring guise, it didn't sell well, and Ducati waited until 1997 to release a replacement (the ST2).

The 900 Monster of 1993 took the 900 Supersport engine, and when placed in an 888-derived chassis created a new niche naked motorcycle. The Monster went on to become an extremely successful model for Ducati, and the early examples are still great bikes. The 900S versions were higher spec and particularly appealing.

906 Paso, 907 ie 120%
900 Supersport, 900 Monster 150%
900 Superlight 200%

The 1989 900 Supersport signalled a return to Ducati's sporting roots, but was let down by the Weber carburettor.

From 1990 the 900 Supersport featured Mikuni carburettors. This is the 1997 version.

The 900 Monster first appeared in 1994 and proved exceptionally popular, establishing a cult line-up that continues today.

The 907 ie was a short-lived attempt at sustaining the Paso concept.

1990-2001 smaller twins: 350/400/600/750 Monster and Supersport
Although Ducati released the 900 with a new 'large' crankcase design, the smaller Pantah-derived five-speed engine continued throughout the 1990s in the Monster and Supersport. This engine wasn't as strong as the six-speed 900, and there were various types of wet or dry clutches fitted. Earlier versions generally only had

a single front disc brake and a steel swingarm. Later types were more similar to the 900, with an aluminium swingarm and twin front disc brakes. If power isn't an issue, these bikes are very similar to the larger displacement versions, and considerably cheaper.

120%

The 400 Supersport was very similar to the 600 and 750, but for the smaller engine. This 1994 version has a steel swingarm, wet clutch and single front disc brake.

The 750 Monster of 2001 was the final version with Mikuni carburettors.

1998-2002 900 ie 750 ie Supersport, Sport, Monster, MHe, ST2

The first new model released after the infusion of money by the Texas Pacific Group was the Terblanche-designed 900 fuel-injected Supersport of 1998. Although this resulted in a small boost in horsepower, and an improvement in ride-ability, the Terblanche Supersport provided a much less comfortable riding position than its predecessor. Offered with either a full or half fairing, the styling didn't really catch on either. Soon afterwards a 750 version was available, and, in 2001, the Monster was fuel-injected. For 2002, a more basic 900 Sport was available.

In 1997 the ST2 arrived, Ducati's first Sport Tourer since the 907 ie With a water-cooled, two-valve, fuel-injected engine in an 888-derived chassis, the ST2 was an excellent bike. For the first time on a Ducati, dedicated luggage was also available. These are comfortable long-distance bikes, but they don't hold their value well.

The 2001 900 MHe (Mike Hailwood evoluzione) was an attempt to recreate the legend of the bevel-drive Mike

Styled by Pierre Terblanche, the 900 Supersport wasn't a great success.

Hailwood Replica. Although the 900 ie engine was shared with the Supersport, everything else was new, including the frame. For some reason Ducati penny-pinched by fitting basic non-adjustable suspension, but, as only around 2000 were produced, the 900 MHe remains a rare, and quite collectable, model.

900 ie 750 ie Supersport, Sport
130-140%
900 ie Monster 140%
ST2 120%
900 MHe 300%

The 900 Monster gained fuel-injection in 2001.

ST2s are great sport touring bikes.

One of the more collectable modern Ducatis is the limited edition 900 MHe.

2002-07 620, 800, Supersport, Sport, Monster, Multistrada, S2R

An updated 620cc engine was released in the Monster for 2002, growing to 800cc and joining the SS range for 2003. These models had improved clutches, and the 800 gained ten more horsepower over the 750, and a six-speed gearbox. All these models were fuel-injected, and the 800 Sport and Supersport were discontinued after 2004. The 800cc engine subsequently lived from 2005 in the appealing Monster S2R, and the 620 lasted until 2007 when the 695 replaced it. By 2008 the 800 had also disappeared. These smaller models are all unappreciated, offering a similar riding experience and performance to later versions, but at a more affordable price.

620, 800 Supersport, Sport, Monster,
Multistrada 120%
800 S2R 130%

Only available for 2003 and 2004, the 800 Supersport replaced the earlier 750.

The S2R was one of the most appealing Monsters.

The 620 Multistrada lasted only for 2006, the concept of a small engine in a large motorcycle not really hitting the mark.

2003-2010 1000 DS Multistrada, Monster, Hypermotard, Supersport, Sport Classic

The next generation Desmodue arrived in 2003 with the Dual Spark 1000. Updates to the top and bottom ends saw an increase in horsepower and improved cooling. The engine initially appeared in the Monster and Supersport, and in 2004 the new Multistrada. The Multistrada was possibly the best all-round bike Ducati had produced. With the demise of the Supersport after 2005, the Dual Spark engine continued in the 2006 SportClassic range. These initially included three models: the Paul Smart Replica, Sport 1000, and GT 1000. Although the SportClassics were not especially popular when new, they are now more appreciated. The SportClassic was also the last model to feature the 1000 DS engine.

1000 DS Multistrada, Monster, Hypermotard, Supersport, Sport 200%
PS 1000 300%
1000 S 250%
GT 1000 220%

Another short-lived model was the 1000 DS Supersport. This was the final model in the venerable Supersport line-up that began back in 1974.

The GT 1000 was the longest-running Sport Classic, finally finishing in 2010.

The Sport 1000 S is becoming increasingly popular.

This limited edition NCR recreation of the 1977 Daytona Superbike race winner is extremely rare and expensive.

2004- 2007 ST3, ST3S

For 2004 a new version of the water-cooled, single overhead camshaft engine appeared in the form of the Desmotre. With 992cc shared with the 1000 DS, but with two intake valves and a single exhaust, the Desmotre produced 102 horsepower, close to the more complex Desmoquattro. This engine only appeared in the Sport Touring series, initially replacing the ST2, and, by 2006, the ST3S replaced the ST4S in the line-up. Unfortunately, despite the excellence of the three-valve engine in the Sport Touring chassis it suffered the fate of many earlier Ducatis of this genre. By 2008 the Sport Touring range was no longer available.

ST3 150%
ST3S 170%

2006-2013 695, 696, 796 Monster, Hypermotard

A new generation of smaller displacement engines was initiated with the 695 in 2006, and evolved into the next generation Monster, the 696, in 2008. These engines all featured a slipper clutch, and were generally more

Although largely forgotten, the ST3 three-valve was arguably the finest of the Sport Touring series.

The Monster 696 was the first of a new generation.

refined than earlier versions. For 2010 a 796cc version joined the range, initially as the Hypermotard, and in 2011 the Monster. The 796 was a particularly nicely balanced engine, producing a respectable 87 horsepower in the Monster. However, as with many mid-range Ducatis, they tend to get overlooked in favour of the larger displacement versions.
120%-150%

2007-2013 1100, 1100S Multistrada, Hypermotard, Monster, Monster Diesel
The gradual increase in capacity of the air-cooled, two-valve engine culminated in the 1100cc version, first available in the Multistrada of 2007. By 2008 it was powering the Hypermotard, and by 2009 a 95 horsepower version was in the Monster. The highest power version was the Monster Diesel, the air-cooled engine finally breaking the 100 horsepower barrier. Several higher specification versions, such as the EVO, were also available.
1100 Multistrada, Hypermotard, Monster 150%-170%
1100 EVO versions 180%-200%

The 1100cc Desmodue engine first appeared in the Multistrada.

5 Before you view

– be well informed

To avoid a wasted journey, and the disappointment of discovering that the bike doesn't match your expectations, it'll help to be clear about the questions you want to ask before you pick up the phone. Some of these points might appear basic, but when you're excited about the prospect of buying your dream bike, it's amazing how some of the most obvious things slip the mind. You should also check the current values in the motorcycle magazine classifieds and on the Internet.

Where is the bike?

Is it going to be worth travelling to the next county/state, or even across a border? Finding a machine locally is always the easiest option, as viewing will not be so difficult. Although the machine may not sound as interesting, you can add to your knowledge with very little effort, so make a visit – it might even be better than you expect.

Cost of collection and delivery?

A dealer may be used to quoting for delivery. A private owner may agree to meet you halfway, but only agree to this after you have seen the bike at the vendor's address to validate the documents. Conversely, you could meet halfway and agree the sale, but insist on meeting at the vendor's address for the handover.

Dealer or private sale?

Establish early on if the bike is being sold by its owner or by a trader. A private owner should know the history of the bike, so don't be afraid to ask detailed questions. A dealer may have more limited knowledge of the bike's history, but may have some documentation. A dealer may offer a warranty or guarantee (ask for a printed copy).

View – when and where?

It's always preferable to view the bike at the vendor's home or business premises. Always arrange viewing in daylight, preferably when it isn't raining (a damp sheen can hide blemishes, and a test ride is probably not available). Make sure you view the bike at the address printed on the ownership documents. Avoid anybody who only provides a mobile phone contact number and who insists on bringing the bike to you or meeting at a public location.

Reason for sale?

Make this one of your first questions. Why is the bike being sold, and how long has it been with the current owner? How many previous owners?

Condition?

Ask for an honest appraisal of the bike's condition. Ask specifically about some of the check items described in Chapter 8.

All original specification?

Unlike an older classic Ducati, all original specification isn't such an issue with a

Desmodue. Sensible additions, such as factory options, could actually increase the value. Apart from the collectable limited edition versions, virtually every one of these bikes will have been modified in some way. If they are official Ducati Performance items (such as exhausts, brakes, suspension, clutch, etc), the owner could have spent a great deal of money without any hope of a return. Look at the type of aftermarket modification, and ask to see documentation.

Matching data/legal ownership?

Frame and engine numbers are discussed more thoroughly later, but always ask the seller if they are clearly visible and match the paperwork. Is the owner's name and address recorded in the official registration documents?

For those countries that require an annual test of roadworthiness, does the bike have a document showing it complies (an MoT certificate in the UK can be verified on 0845 600 5977)?

Does the bike carry a current road fund licence/licence plate tag? If not, in the UK it should have a SORN (Statutory Off Road Notification) certificate.

Does the vendor own the bike outright? Money might be owed to a finance company or bank, the bike could even be stolen. Several organisations will supply data on ownership, based on the bike's licence plate number; for a fee. Such companies can also often tell you if the bike has been 'written-off' by an insurance company. In the UK the following organisations can supply vehicle data:

HPI – 01722 422 422 – www.hpicheck.com
AA – 0870 600 0836 – www.theaa.com
RAC – 0870 533 3660 – www.rac.co.uk

Other countries will have similar organisations.

Insurance

Check with your existing insurer before setting out – your current policy might not cover you if you buy the bike and decide to ride it home.

How can you pay?

A pocketful of cash can be a useful lever when bargaining over the final price. Personal cheques take several days to clear, but a banker's draft (a cheque issued by a bank) in the current owner's name is as good as cash, but safer. Electronic bank transfers are becoming the fastest and most reliable method to transfer payments, and are particularly useful for overseas transactions.

Buying at auction?

If the intention is to buy at auction see Chapter 10 for further advice.

Professional vehicle check (mechanical examination)

There are often marque/model specialists who will undertake professional examination of a vehicle on your behalf. Owners' clubs may be able to put you in touch with such specialists.

– these items will really help

Before you rush out of the door, gather together a few items that will help as you work your way around the bike.

This book
This book is designed to be your guide at every step, so take it along and use the check boxes in chapter 9 – *Serious evaluation* to help you assess each area of the bike. Don't be afraid to let the seller see you using it.

Reading glasses (if you need them for close work)
Taking your reading glasses if you need them to read documents and make close up inspections.

Taking these items with you when you go to view a potential purchase not only helps you to better assess the bike, but also shows the seller that you mean business.

Overalls
Be prepared to get dirty. Take along a pair of overalls, if you have them.

Digital camera
A digital camera is handy so that later you can study some areas of the bike more closely. Take a picture of any part of the bike that causes you concern, and seek an expert opinion.

Compression tester
A compression tester is easy to use. It screws into the sparkplug holes and measures the compression as you spin the engine over on the starter. Remember to remove both sparkplugs.

A friend, preferably a knowledgeable enthusiast
Ideally, have a friend or knowledgeable enthusiast come along with you to see the bike – a second opinion is always worth having.

7 15-minute evaluation
– walk away or stay?

General condition
First impressions count. Does the bike look well cared for or neglected? Damaged nuts and Allen bolts are a sign of a less than sympathetic owner. Check for signs of crash damage – are the pegs, silencer, forks, or handlebar ends scraped on one side of the bike? If they are, ask the seller how it happened. At the steering head, check whether the steering stops are bent or dented; a sure sign of an accident.

Try pushing the bike forward a few metres, and back again. It should roll freely on a flat surface – if it doesn't, it's likely the brake calipers are sticking and will need to be stripped and cleaned, or replaced.

What aftermarket parts are fitted? Aftermarket parts are very popular for these bikes, but you should check that they're legal (the exhaust, for example). With regard to later bikes, it's also important to ascertain if an aftermarket exhaust is accompanied by the appropriate fuel-injection modifications. Carbon-fibre replacement body parts are also extremely popular, but they deteriorate markedly when exposed to water and sun. A recent phenomenon is for owners to sell off the high-priced aftermarket items that were once on the bike. Aftermarket parts are typically worth more if sold off the bike instead of left on. If the good aftermarket parts are on the bike, ask the owner if the stock parts are available. Remember, today's commonplace bikes are tomorrow's classics, and classics are more valuable if they are in original and stock condition.

It's worth remembering that a tatty-looking bike may well be perfectly sound underneath – something that should become clear during the test ride. A scruffy appearance should be reflected in the price, though.

Engine/frame numbers
Do the VINs (Vehicle Identification Numbers) tally with those on the documentation? If they don't you may just be looking at a bike which has had an engine swap that was never recorded in the paperwork, or it could have been built up from stolen parts. If the owner doesn't have a convincing explanation, go home – there are plenty of Desmodues on the market.

Documentation
Make sure that the seller is actually who he or she says they are by checking the registration document. In the UK this is the V5C. The person listed on the document isn't necessarily the legal owner, but the details should match those of whomever is selling the bike. Also use the V5C to verify the engine/frame numbers.

An annual roadworthiness certificate – the MoT in the UK – is handy proof that the bike was roadworthy when tested. A whole sheaf of them gives evidence of the bike's history, when it was actively being used, and what the mileage was. The more of these that come with the bike the better.

Engine
Start the engine, from cold if possible. Does the starter engage cleanly? If it just spins over without engaging at all, or makes a 'clunking' noise, then the starter sprag clutch is worn out. Start it up and notice the degree to which you have to

use the choke to keep it running. Also notice the state of idle and, by placing a screwdriver blade on the valve cover and listening with your ear at the handle, you can discern any unusual cacophony from the valve-train. Run the engine through the rev range to check the ease at which the gearbox shifts.

Suspension/tyres

Check the front forks for oil leaks, pitting, or rusting. Take the bike off the stand, hold the front brake and pump the forks up and down – they should move smoothly and without squeaks or rattles. Sit on the bike to check the rear suspension; the shock should move smoothly and quietly. If it feels over-soft (bearing in mind the spring pre-load setting) then it could need replacing.

Tyres are easy to check, and well-worn rubber is a good means of levering down the price. Look for a flat worn in the centre of the rear tyre – this upsets the handling and means you'll have to replace the tyre soon.

Specials like this, with a two-valve engine in a 999 chassis, can represent a good buy second-hand because of a limited market.

First impressions count, but take a close look, too.

Many Desmodues will include aftermarket exhaust systems.

Tyre condition is easy to assess.

Look for signs of crash damage. It's likely an older, high mileage bike will have been dropped at some point in its life, if only at low speed. If there is evidence, think about this on the test ride – is the bike running straight and true, even when braking?

One problem affecting many of these bikes is a leaking clutch slave cylinder. Early versions were particularly prone to failure.

Does the starter motor work first time? If it makes a screeching noise during starting then the sprag clutch is probably slipping. Best tested when the engine is cold, as it may not show up when it's warm. The solution will require replacement of the sprag bearing and possibly the starter gear.

Brake calipers will stick if used through the winter and not cleaned. The cast iron discs on earlier models also rust.

Engine paint can flake off, allowing the alloy to corrode. Even if it looks unsightly, it may still be a mechanically fine motorcycle, but it may be more difficult to resell, so expect price to reflect appearance.

– 30 minutes for years of enjoyment

Score each section as follows: 4=excellent; 3=good; 2=average; 1=poor. The totting up procedure is detailed at the end of the chapter. Be realistic in your marking!

Engine and frame numbers

The first job is to check whether the VIN (Vehicle Identification Number) for engine and frame tally with those on the documentation. If they don't, make your excuses and walk away. The VIN is stamped on the right side of the steering head, the engine number is located on the left side of the engine, just below the water pump.

Identifying the actual model from the VIN can be a challenge, but can also aid in determining the authenticity of limited edition models. Post-1980 US models and post-2002 non-US models have a 17-character VIN as follows:

Characters 1-3:   World manufacturer code (Z = Italy, D = Ducati, M = motorcycle)
Character 4:   1 = Street version
Character 5:   Motorcycle model: D = Paso; G = 750 F1; H = homologation model; K = 750 Sport; L = Supersport; M = 907 ie; N = 750SS; P = E900 Elefant; R = Monster; T = Sport Touring; V = Multistrada; W = SportClassic
Character 6:   Engine type: A = Air-cooled twin; B = Liquid-cooled twin; C = Air/oil-cooled twin
Character 7:   Engine displacement: 2 = 600cc; 3 = 750cc; 3 = Australian 1996 900SS; 4 = 900cc; 8 = 1000cc
Character 8:   Net brake horsepower: H = 750 Sport; K = 600 620 SS; L = E900 Elefant, Monster 750; M = 750SS, 750 F1; N = Paso, 907 ie, 900SS, Monster 900, MH900e; P = ST2, Monster 1000, Multistrada
Character 9:   Check digit (a calculated number that is used to verify the validity of the VIN. This is a single number or the letter X)
Character 10:   Model year code: 9 = 1979; A = 1980; B = 1981; C = 1982; D = 1983; E = 1984; F = 1985; G = 1986; H = 1987; J = 1988; K = 1989; L = 1990; M = 1991; N = 1992; P = 1993; R = 1994; S = 1995; T = 1996; V = 1997; W = 1998; X = 1999; Y = 2000; 1 = 2001; 2 = 2002; 3 = 2003; 4 = 2004; 5 = 2005; 6 = 2006; 7 = 2007; 8 = 2008; 9 = 2009; K = 1989; L = 1990; M = 1991; N = 1992; P = 1993; R = 1994; S = 1995; T = 1996; V = 1997; W = 1998; X = 1999; Y = 2000; 1 = 2001; 2 = 2002; 3 = 2003; 4 = 2004; 5 = 2005; 6 = 2006; 7 = 2007; 8 = 2008; 9 = 2009; A = 2010; B = 2011; C = 2012; D = 2013
Character 11:   Manufacturing plant code: B = Bologna, Italy; V = Varese, Italy (Cagivas)
Characters 12-17: Production number (six-digit sequential)

Prior to 2002, non-US models were assigned a 17-character VIN that does not incorporate the US and post-2002 European character arrangement, but this website can aid identification; http://www.motoverse.com/tools/vin/ducati.asp.

VIN plates vary from country to country, as do VIN numbers.

Most bikes will have a frame number stamped on the steering head.

Paint, alloy, plastic, chrome, fasteners   ④ ③ ② ①

Over the years Ducati's finish has improved dramatically. The paintwork on Desmodues is generally good, and the plastic bodywork tough. The bodywork can benefit from a layer of protection, such as 3M's clear film layer. This is particularly effective in protecting the leading edge of the fairing, and the chin fairing behind the front wheel. These two areas receive the most abuse during riding, and paint

Engine cases will deteriorate if not looked after.

Original paint on fork legs was never very durable.

If a bike has been well cared for this will be obvious.

Original fasteners rust easily.

damage here can indicate the general level of care. The fuel tank is also prone to scratching from belt buckles, but can be protected by tank pads or a full tank wrap. Look for bungee cord marks on the tail section.

The zinc plating on OEM fasteners and bolts is still very thin. Routine cleaning will remove the zinc plate, revealing the colour of the bolt, and this looks unsightly, particularly on the frame, wheel and engine bolts. Plain alloy parts will corrode if not washed regularly, and the painted engine cases can flake badly on earlier models. Rust on the bike, particularly engine bolts and exhaust header pipes, is another sign of neglect. Chrome plating has never been a Ducati strong point, so look underneath all visible chrome parts for signs of pitting. If the bike has been exposed to the elements, the black plastic parts may have aged prematurely.

Bodywork/mudguards

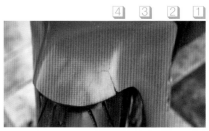

Standard bodywork is tough but will break in a crash. Check for mudguard damage.

In one respect, buying a second-hand bike is far easier than purchasing a used car – for one thing there's far less bodywork to worry about. The quality of the Desmodue bodywork is good, but it will still suffer if the bike has been dropped. Although scratches can be painted out, cracks are difficult to repair. The other consideration is the cost of genuine bodywork. Unless it has been replaced after a crash by an insurance pay-out, aftermarket fibreglass or carbon parts may have replaced genuine bodywork. This isn't necessarily a bad thing. The stock plastic bodywork on fully-faired models is quite heavy, and also has considerable sound/heat absorbing material glued inside. But aftermarket bodywork will detract from the ultimate value of the bike.

Frame sliders/crash bungs can protect the bike in a fall.

For some models, particularly early Pantahs and 750 F1s, finding genuine replacement bodywork is now getting difficult. Look for frame sliders/crash bungs and bar end sliders to protect the bike in a fall, and check for general fairing and mudguard damage. Mutilated bodywork is indicative of a careless owner. Damaged bodywork could also indicate more serious damage elsewhere on the bike, so treat it as a clue to look for more bad news, such as bent or snapped footpegs and levers, and scraped silencers. Look for non-standard and ill-fitting bodywork, as

Check for cracks in fibreglass bodywork.

this will generally devalue the motorcycle. Windshields can also become cracked or pitted.

Many bikes will probably have some aftermarket carbon-fibre components. This may include swingarm protectors, rear wheel huggers, front and inner rear mudguards, and a range of smaller shields (rear master cylinder, etc). All carbon-fibre componentry is costly as the material is expensive to mould, and the best carbon-fibre includes a clear protective coating over the resin as a seal. Even the best carbon-fibre can degrade if exposed to harsh sunlight and excess water, so look for yellowing and fading. It is not easy to restore discoloured carbon-fibre.

Safety regulations require a large rear mudguard, and, as the stock rear mudguard is rather bulbous and unsightly, a mudguard or fender eliminator will have replaced many, particularly on Monsters. The stock rear mudguard can be removed and replaced by a bracket that secures the turn signals and tail-light. This is generally not a problem as the rear end will look cleaner, but on the Monsters many owners simply trim the large stock mudguard. This will lower the bike's resale value. On the ST series, eliminating the rear mudguard will result in water spray covering the back of the bike. Finally, have a good look over the bike for missing screws and fasteners. These always seem to get loose and fall out.

Decals/graphics [4] [3] [2] [1]

Because of the pride of ownership of the name, decals and badges are an important aspect of any Ducati. The decals on Desmodue Ducatis all last well because they are covered by a clear coating. Check the model has the correct graphics, as these sometimes changed from one model year to the next.

Decal fonts changed over time. This is the pre-1986 Giugiaro graphic.

Original decals last well.

Seat [4] [3] [2] [1]

Most Desmodues had a dual seat, with only the early 750 F1, 900 SL, 900 MHe and some of the SportClassics having a single seat. Monster and Sport Touring seats were more generous in padding. All are moulded rubber, some with a plastic cover, and shouldn't deteriorate unless they are ripped or crack. A split seat cover is particularly annoying, as it will allow the foam to soak up water (and it never seems to dry out). The stock seat pad is prone to wear, and this can give an indication as to the actual mileage of the bike. Check the storage compartment underneath the seat for an owner's manual and tool kit.

Although the stock seat on most Desmodues is nicely finished, it's hard and uncomfortable, and the angle causes the rider to slide forward. An aftermarket seat will not detract too much from the value of the bike, and may enhance rider comfort. Sargent and Corbin offer excellent alternative seats for all models. Sargent replacement seats are light (a little more than a kilogram) and colour coordinated, the underside of the Monster seat providing a large storage compartment. Corbin seats are similar, ergonomically designed in high density foam to disperse the rider's weight across a greater area. This reduces the tendency for the rider to slide into the tank. The tail section retains its standard hinging action, with stock mounts.

Standard seats are not known for their comfort, but are nicely finished and durable.

Most seats, even when more than 20 years old like this one, are still intact.

Rubbers

A good guide to the mileage on a second-hand car is wear on the pedal rubbers, and the same goes for a bike. In this case look at footpeg, gearlever, and handlebar grips. Although most modern bike footpegs don't have rubbers, the standard soft handgrips can provide a guide. Well worn rubbers can indicate a high mileage, which may or may not concur with what the mileometer indicates or the owner claims! Of course, rubbers can be replaced so this is not an infallible method – look for suspiciously new rubbers on an otherwise well-used bike.

The condition of the gearshift rubber is a good indication of the amount of use.

The condition of the handgrips indicates wear or crash damage.

Frame and swingarm

The most important job here is to check whether the frame is straight and true. Crash damage may have bent it, putting the wheels out of line. One way of checking is by using an experienced eye and a taut string, but the surest way to ascertain frame straightness is on the test ride – any serious misalignment will be obvious in the handling.

If the bike pulls to one side, or you need to put more force on one bar than the other to keep the bike in a straight line, then the frame could be bent. The same applies if it appears to corner better in one direction than the other. There should be no wobbles or weaves, whether in a straight line at speed or when cornering.

As it usually takes the full force of a front-end impact, the headstock is a key place to look for crash damage. If the paint is flaking off here, but the rest of the frame paint is fine, then ask the owner why. All these bikes have tubular steel frames that are susceptible to cracks around the steering head after a front-end collision. Inspect the steering stops. Bent stops indicate the bike has been down at some stage. On Supersports prior to 1997 the frame tubing to the steering head was thinner, so look for cracks on earlier models.

With crash damage in mind, check the whole bike. Most Desmodues have excellent ground clearance, so scrapes on the footpegs probably indicate more than enthusiastic riding. Recently replaced footpegs and mirrors are also suspicious. Check that the handlebars

Check the steering head for damage and flaking paint. Early Supersports like this had thinner tubing around the steering head.

Check the frame for damage and flaking paint. On models with a cantilever aluminium swingarm look for cracks at the shock mount.

are straight and pointing in the right direction. Are the mirrors damaged or have they been replaced? The standard mirrors on sporting models are basically useless as mirrors, and are vulnerable in a crash. On Supersports, if you can, remove the fairing so the frame and engine can be inspected. While fairings add to the visual impact of a bike, they can also hide evidence of frame and engine damage. Look for damage to the oil cooler, and frame mounting points for the fairing. New brackets could indicate the bike has had a crash, and the brackets have been replaced. Dented wheel rims may also indicate that the frame is bent. Unless you're sure the frame hasn't been damaged, you should factor the expense of frame straightening into the price.

Aluminium swingarms on earlier models were also prone to cracking, and 1989-90 Sports were recalled to replace the aluminium swingarm with a steel type. All aluminium cantilever swingarms can crack near the shock mount.

Stands

Only the Pantahs, F1s and ST-series were fitted with a centre stand as well as a side stand, and it aids chain lubrication and adjustment. Eventually the stand pivots will wear, so if you're looking at a Pantah or ST, heave the bike on the stand on firm ground, and try twisting it from side to side – it shouldn't move. On an ST you are unlikely to find a worn centre stand, as most owners will use the more convenient side stand day-to-day.

As all side stands have quite a bit of weight to support, check it isn't loose or bent. The stands can bend if owners sit on the bike when it is supported by the side stand. The stand simply wasn't designed to take this weight, however slim the rider!

Bike stands are a necessary accessory for most maintenance efforts on all Desmodues except the Pantah, F1, and ST. Ask if the owners had access to a stand, or if one comes with the sale. If the owner hasn't had access to a bike stand it is unlikely the chain has been correctly tensioned.

Centre stands are useful for chain lubrication and adjustment, but the bike shouldn't wobble when on the stand.

The side stand should be secure and straight. This one has been lengthened.

Electrics and fuel-injection

If there is one thing that scares away potential owners from a Ducati it is the possibility of electrical problems. The main cause of electrical problems is battery failure. Ducatis like fully charged batteries, and any bike sitting for more than a week should be placed on a battery trickle charger. Pre-2001 models had the older wet cell YB16AL-A2 battery, and these can short out, causing damage to the solenoid, regulator and coils. Ducati fuel-injection systems require significant battery charge, and won't work satisfactorily with a weak battery. Most Ducati charging systems include a warning light to indicate when the voltage is low. Check this light is not on when the engine is running, as this indicates the battery is nearly dead. Another sign of impending electrical malfunction is fuel-injection 'hiccupping.'

Early Desmodues had a single-phase alternator, usually 350 watts, that was fully taxed by just the horn and headlight. The 1998 ST2 had a more powerful 400 watt alternator, and, in 1999, Ducati switched to a three-phase 520 watt alternator and voltage regulator (without the warning light). This reduced most charge related problems.

The wiring harness is a tough two-piece design on these bikes, even the 35-year old early Pantahs have few problems here, but the harness connector is susceptible to water ingress and hence corrosion. Check for loose or frayed wiring, and rusty or corroded connectors. Corroded connectors can signify impending electrical problems. It is particularly important the cable connections to the generator and voltage regulator, starter to solenoid, and solenoid to battery are all clean. Corroded or loose connectors attaching the generator to the voltage regulator are responsible for many blown regulators. All earlier single-phase (pre-1999) regulators were more prone to failure than the later type. The first sign

Headlight styles vary. This is the mid-1980s rectangular type.

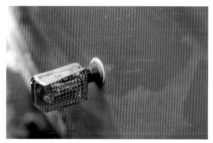

Make sure everything works.

Look for aftermarket wiring, like this fuse box.

of a regulator problem will be a blinking charge light. Many early bikes will have had a regulator fail at some point in their life, so check if the replacement is genuine or aftermarket. Although aftermarket regulators are considerably cheaper than original units, most are inferior to the updated genuine Ducati regulators. The installation of an aftermarket LCD voltmeter indicates a conscientious owner.

Run the bike and check that all the lights and turn signals work. The Ducati's charging system is marginal, and has a difficult time maintaining charge at idle. The headlight and turn signal connectors have been known to melt and even catch on fire. Check that the headlight is not a more powerful aftermarket type, as this will result in charging problems. Also check that the bike doesn't have a US-style left handlebar switch without a headlight on/off button. If it does, budget on replacing it with a Euro-style switch. Next, check that all the warning lights are operational. If

Euro-style switches with an on/off headlight are preferred.

the neutral light switch has shorted out, this can cause some electrical problems (and it is difficult to remove for repair). A failed oil pressure sensor can provide an erroneous oil pressure indication.

Although Ducati used five series of ECU – the P7, P8, 1.6, 1.5 and 5.9 – the P7 was only fitted to the 907 ie, and the 1.6 on the Gran Canyon and ST2. The 1.5 debuted on the SS ie and Monster (until 2001), with the 5.9 on subsequent models. More recent Monsters have a Siemens ECU. With the exception of the Siemens, all have been known to fail. As the P7 is now quite old, availability of replacement parts is limited. Check that the bike comes with two keys, particularly models with a 5.9 ECU. As the 5.9 ECU is mated to the immobiliser system, if you lose your keys you will have to replace not only the ignition, but also the instrument panel and ECU. Sensor failure can be a problem. If the throttle position sensor fails, replacement is an expensive proposition. Throttle sensor failure is immediately evident when riding the bike, as low speed running is very erratic.

The original ignition coils are robust and rarely fail, but pick-up coils do occasionally. Ominous signs here are 'hiccupping' at sustained rpm, or the engine dying at high rpm. Testing with a voltmeter requires removal of the right-hand engine side cover. Additional ignition problems can be caused by deterioration of the original sparkplug wires, the symptoms similar to that of coil malfunction.

Hesitating during starting is an indication of a dying battery or worn starter sprag. Starter solenoids, and the associated fuses, can also fail if they have suffered a voltage spike. When checking a bike's electrical system, you should first ensure that everything works as it should, and that the electrical components are stock. Aftermarket ,additions such as high output coils, fuel pressure modifiers and ignition amplifiers, will tax the already challenged standard electrical system. Another challenge to the electrical system is a blocked fuel filter. If the fuel pump has to run excessively hard to overcome a filter restriction, the fuel pump relay can blow, and the alternator wiring and regulator can overheat.

Other potential electrical problems include the side stand interrupt circuit (on post-1999 models) and the electrical wheel speedometer sensor (post 2000 Monsters and post 2003 other models).

Wheels/tyres

Most Desmodues were fitted with cast alloy 17-inch wheels, but there were exceptions. Pantahs had 18-inch wheels, 750 F1s and Pasos 16-inch front and sometimes rear, and the SportClassic series 17-inch spoked wheels with alloy rims. From 1989 the Supersport and Monster had three-spoke aluminium Brembo wheels. The rim sizes (3.50- and 5.50-inch) are still suitable for the latest tyres, but these wheels are soft and prone to distortion if ridden fast over potholes. These wheels really need to be checked for runout with both wheels on a stand. If you do have access to front and rear wheelstands check both wheels for trueness, bends, and nicks from careless tyre removal and installation.

During the 2000s, five-spoke Marchesini (also made by Brembo) replaced the earlier three-spoke items. These were considerably lighter (by 2kg on each wheel) and are a popular upgrade for the earlier three-spoke Brembos. The only thing to check with wheel upgrades is the use of the correct axle. 17mm axles featured until 1993, and 19mm from 1994.

Many Desmodues are used as high-performance sports bikes or the basis of a custom, and a common modification is the replacement of the heavy stock wheels with lighter aftermarket magnesium, or magnesium carbon/composite. These wheels are expensive, and if you're looking at a bike with aftermarket rims this should be reflected in the price. It may work in your favour, but always ask if the stock wheels are also available.

Apart from the Sport Touring series most Desmoquattros are not used for touring, so wheel bearing failure is rare. They don't last forever, though, and as it's difficult to inspect the double-sealed wheel bearings for wear, use the mileage as a guide. Wheel bearings should be replaced every 20-25,000 miles (30-40,000km).

Tyre life varies according to riding style, but these are high horsepower motorcycles and none are particularly light on tyres. Look at the type of wear on the rear tyre. A flat worn in the centre with little wear on the sides indicates a lot of high-speed motorway use, and less than 50% remaining tread is a useful bargaining tool. Are the tyres worn right round, or is the edge of the tread untouched by tarmac? The former suggests a hard rider but this isn't necessarily bad if the bike is well looked after. Look at the front tyre. If it's cupped or unevenly worn, this could indicate that the wheel is out of balance, or the steering head bearings are worn. Check the tyre pressures. Improper inflation can drastically affect the handling and accelerate tyre wear. Tyre brand comes

A wheel bearing check is relatively easy, but wear is difficult to gauge.

Check alloy rims for corrosion and dents.

Less than 50 per cent remaining tyre tread can be a useful bargaining tool.

Some of the higher spec models, like this Hypermotard 1100S, have extremely light, forged Marchesini wheels.

SportClassics had wire-spoked wheels.

down to personal choice and the type of riding envisaged. Older bikes with 16- and 18-inch wheels have a much more limited tyre choice.

Steering head bearings

Loose steering head bearings will cause the front-end to shake, and this not only affects the handling but will destroy the bearings, too. It's important to check the steering head before buying a bike, as replacing the steering head bearings is a major job, requiring removal of the fork legs and a special nut-tightening tool. Depending on the model, the steering head bearings on the Desmodue are either tapered roller bearings or plain ball bearings in a plastic cup. With the ball bearing type each bearing has a sealing ring and the lower seal has a tendency to retain water if the bike is frequently washed or ridden in the rain.

Ideally the front of the bike should be elevated so as to swing the handlebars from lock to lock. If there is any roughness or stiffness this could indicate lack of grease, or bearing failure. To check for looseness, put the steering on full lock, grip the base of the forks and try rocking them back and forth. If there is movement at the fork clamp, then the steering head bearings are loose. This may simply mean the steering head nut may need to be re-torqued to keep the races tight in the bearing housings, but it could also mean the bearings are dented and need to be replaced. It's easy to confuse movement here with play in the forks. When testing the forks by pumping them up and down, any movement in the steering head could indicate the bearings need attention. If it requires further investigation – either bring in an expert, take the bike to a dealer, or walk away. Alternatively, show the movement to the owner and use it as a bargaining tool.

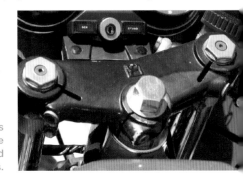

The condition of steering head bearings affects handling. Early Pantahs like this had tapered roller steering head bearings.

Swingarm bearings

Swingarm bearings are of concern primarily on the single-sided swingarm models with eccentric adjustment. These needle bearings are often neglected, and if the bike is ridden in wet or salty conditions and the bearings aren't regularly lubricated, these can fail prematurely. The swingarm bearings on dual-sided swingarms should also be lubricated regularly, but as removal of the swingarm pin is difficult, this is unlikely. Check for swingarm endplay by tugging the swingarm from side-to-side. This is difficult unless the bike is on a stand.

Front forks

As the production period for Desmodues encompasses more than 30 years, the fork types varied considerably. Early Pantahs had a standard 35mm Marzocchi or Paioli, with F1s receiving 38 or 40mm Marzocchi or Forcella Italia. All these forks are quite basic in operation and design, and the only real problem could be oil leaks from the seals. Apart from a few models with a Marzocchi M1R fork, all the forks after 1991 were inverted Showa, Marzocchi or Öhlins. The inverted forks, particularly with exposed fork stanchions, can suffer from oil leaks around the seals. Look at the condition of the fork stanchion. Any imperfections to the outer wall can damage a fork seal and cause an oil leak. Also inspect the dust seal around the bottom of the stanchion. These can rot if the bike is ridden a lot in the rain or left in strong sunlight.

Check the forks for wear, ideally with the front wheel elevated. This is easier on the Pantahs, F1s and ST series with a centre stand. Look for any movement by grasping the bottom of the forks and trying to rock the fork legs back and forth. Check the fork legs visually to see if they are parallel – that is, appear to be on the

Ensure the fork action is smooth.

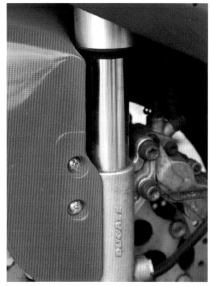

Exposed fork sliders on many models, particularly Monsters, can result in pitted forks and blown oil seals.

same plane when viewed from the side. If they're not they may have been twisted in an accident. Take the bike off the stand, hold on to the front brake and pump up and down. They should move through their whole travel smoothly and freely with no squeaks and rattles. If the suspension feels too soft (difficult to judge without experience) the springs may be worn out.

Check the position of the fork tubes in the top triple clamp. If the forks tubes are raised this will quicken the steering at the expense of high-speed stability. But if more than 3-4 lines on the fork tubes are showing the front wheel can contact the cylinder head during heavy braking. Don't be too concerned if the amount of fork tube protruding from the triple clamp differs left to right. It's more important the fork legs line up at the bottom so the axle doesn't bind.

Rear suspension

Like the front forks, the rear suspension type varied considerably on the Desmodue. Models from the early 1980s featured a traditional twin shock arrangement, later replicated on the SportClassic, while the F1 and Supersport had a monoshock without a linkage, and the Monster, ST and Hypermotard a linkage monoshock. The shock absorber type also varied, with the more highly specified versions featuring an Öhlins item, while others can have a Marzocchi, Paioli, Showa or Sachs. On early models it was common to replace the standard shocks with aftermarket types that generally provided improved damping. As the rear shock is exposed to road debris and grime, check the condition of the shock piston. Most stock shock absorbers are perfectly adequate and don't require periodic maintenance, but may benefit from a rebuild if they have covered a high mileage.

On linkage suspension versions the rear linkage arm chrome ball pivot fittings should be lubricated every 3000 miles. They tend to rust and wear if water is allowed to collect, and are difficult to lubricate, as grease must be forced into the pivot points. Ask the owner when the linkages were last lubricated. Get down on the ground and have a look – do they look clean and well lubed, or are they caked in mud and neglected?

Only a few of the more recent models have a single-sided swingarm.

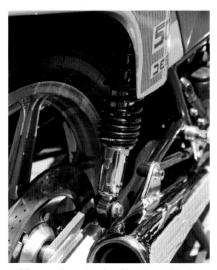

Aftermarket shocks, like these Konis, are a popular alternative to standard Marzocchis or Paiolis on early Pantahs.

On the test ride, seek out the odd manhole cover or pothole – if the suspension feels overly soft and bouncy, then the rear shock (or shocks) may need replacing. While older suspension only had provision for spring preload adjustment, on more modern bikes the rear suspension has myriad settings, and if they are set without care the bike can become almost unrideable. In addition to spring preload, ride height is adjustable, as are compression and rebound damping. Ask the owner if any suspension settings other than stock have been used, and if they were written down.

An Öhlins rear shock absorber was fitted to some limited edition examples.

Steering damper

Steering dampers can be a useful addition to a Desmodue as they help the front end deal with bumps by absorbing fast side-to-side movement. Unlike the Desmoquattro Superbikes, most Desmodues weren't fitted with a steering damper as standard, but aftermarket alternatives are available. As with all aftermarket equipment, adjustable steering dampers (particularly Öhlins) are expensive, and so a good quality unit on the bike adds value.

An aftermarket steering damper is a useful addition to a Desmodue.

Chain/sprockets

With the engine switched off, examine the final drive chain and sprockets. Is the chain clean, well lubed and properly adjusted? Excessive loose or tight spots indicate the chain has stretched. Sit on the bike – there should be around 30mm of play at the mid point of the chain's run. Pulling a link rearward away from the sprocket should only reveal a small portion of the sprocket teeth – any more and it needs replacing. If the sprocket teeth have worn to less than half the thickness of a chain link, it's junk. A chain that's too tight will increase sprocket wear, and can also destroy the output shaft bearing. If the latter fails you'll be stranded and left with a considerable bill for a new output shaft and bearing. A loose chain will cause unnecessary driveline lash, but is preferable to one set too tight.

Check the rear sprocket teeth for wear – if they have a hooked appearance, the sprocket needs replacing. Aluminium sprockets will degrade more quickly than steel. If the rear sprocket needs replacing the countershaft sprocket will too. Countershaft sprockets wear much faster than rear sprockets and are rarely checked because they are hidden behind a plastic plate. If you can, have a look at the countershaft sprocket, as severely worn teeth can shear off. Also check the sprocket securing plate. On pre-2001 models the plate was thinner, and can fail

(the bolts come off or the tabs shear). On a test ride check the clutch action when the engine is hot – if the sprocket rides against the engine casing after the securing plate has come off it the heat generated can boil the clutch fluid. In extreme cases it can punch a hole in the crankcase. Chains and sprockets are not particularly expensive, but there is quite a lot of dismantling time involved.

The chain tensioning system varied from model to model, and some were poorly designed. Check the axle securing plates and adjuster plates for damage. Many are surprisingly fragile and can bend or break if too much torque is applied. Steel adjusters screwed into aluminium were particularly prone to corrosion and breakage. Particularly problematic were the early 1990s Supersports and pre-2002 Monsters and STs.

Clutch

Many types of clutch were fitted to the Desmodue, the Pantahs, 600s, 620s, 750s and 800s having a wet clutch. Most wet clutches were hydraulically-actuated, and after 2005 a slipper clutch was introduced. Pre-2007, larger displacement Desmodues had an hydraulically-actuated dry clutch, noted for its noisy operation. Do not be alarmed by clutch noise, especially when the clutch is activated while the bike is stationary. The friction plate tabs hitting the clutch basket cause the rattle, but if the noise is excessive the plates will need to be replaced. The dry clutch design has some advantages, notably the lack of oil contamination from clutch particles, but also wears more quickly than an oil bath type. More problematic with these bikes is the clutch slave cylinder. Prior to 2000 the slave cylinder included a rubber boot to protect the clutch pushrod and slave cylinder O-ring. This arrangement was unsatisfactory, and, over time, allowed dirt to enter the piston chamber, causing leaks. The slave cylinder design was updated from 2001, and several improved aftermarket products are also available. Check around the slave cylinder, particularly the side stand, for signs of brake fluid damage. If you see peeled paint then there's probably fluid leakage caused by oil ring blow-by in the slave cylinder.

Vented clutch covers may look great, but can allow water to enter the clutch assembly.

Clutch slave cylinder designs have undergone a number of updates. Early examples, like this pre-2001 version, should be checked for leaks.

On a test ride check the clutch is not slipping. A slipping clutch will indicate worn plates, usually as a result of slipping the clutch during take off to compensate for too high gearing. A common modification is an open clutch cover. While this may look racy the clutch is left exposed to crash damage, and if the bike is ridden in the rain the clutch plates will rust and eventually fuse together. From 2003 Ducati fitted aluminium clutch baskets and plates on the ST, and a wet clutch to all 1100 DSs from 2007. The wet clutch makes for a smoother action on the street.

Instruments and switches

Ducati Desmodues were fitted with a variety of instruments, early examples with mechanical speedometers and tachometers, driven by cables. These were Nippon Denso on Pantahs, and Veglia though until 1998. None of these early setups give many problems. Early Monsters didn't have a tachometer but many may have aftermarket arrangements that include a tacho. The ST-series generally had a mechanical speedometer with electronic analogue tachometer. Make sure the tachometer

The Nippon Denso instrument layout of Pantahs was very reliable.

works properly, if it doesn't there could be a problem with the screws at the back, or the connector pins coming loose. Tachometers are designed to work with a particular ECU, and, while they all look similar, replacement is not totally straightforward. The post-2003 Monster had an electrical speedometer with the sensor on the rear brake caliper bracket. These sensors can fail, as can the electronic speedometer. Also check that the warning lights work, and also the switches. Electronic instruments have a downside. As the instrument clusters are circuit-board based, without replacement bulbs, should an idiot light burn out the entire instrument must be replaced.

White-faced Veglia instruments were cable driven through until 1998.

Early Monsters didn't have a tachometer.

The digital dash of later Monsters.

Modern switches should be reliable.

The switchgear on modern Ducatis is industry standard so should be very reliable. If an over enthusiastic jet wash does force water into the switch, a good squirt of WD-40 should get it going again. Check the odometer. Is it working? Does the stated mileage look right, or has the speedo been tampered with? Check the instrument faces. Later versions are plastic and can crack if subjected to prolonged sunlight.

Engine – general impressions

You can tell a lot about the likely condition of a Ducati Desmodue engine without hearing it run. Look for signs of grease or oil on exposed surfaces, particularly around the engine breather assembly. This is notorious for weeping oil at the base, but is more of a problem on pre-99 models. The Desmodue engine needs to be well maintained, with particular attention to oil changes and valve clearances. Check that the oil is clean and the sump not overfilled. An overfilled sump may result in oil blow-by through the oil breather.

A tatty exterior doesn't necessarily mean internal neglect, but watch out for chewed up fasteners where someone has tried to use the wrong size of Allen key. If the fuel smells of shellac the bike has been sitting too long and there could be problems with blocked injectors and fuel filter. Both of these will lead to battery and electrical problems. Beware if a bad smell of fuel and oil permeates the bike.

Exhaust pipes have a tendency to discolour if the mixture is too lean and the engine has overheated. A sooty build up on the exhaust may indicate that the

With the bike upright check that the sump is not overfull.

engine is running too rich. A service history is vital when considering a Desmodue. Valve adjustment, belt replacement and oil change schedules must be adhered to.

Engine – starting/idling

The engine should start promptly and idle smoothly. Don't rely on the neutral light, though, and never push the starter without pulling the clutch first, as the bike could be in gear. Hesitation during starting could indicate a dud battery, and a screeching noise a faulty starter sprag. Mikuni carburettors on pre-1999 models sometimes suffer from a hanging idle, indicating poor carb synchronization or worn jet needles or needle jets. The Mikuni carburettors were dependable, the main problem was float bowl icing in lower temperatures.

There should be no hesitation when the starter button is pressed.

On fuel-injected models a rough idle may mean the injection system requires fine-tuning: the throttle position sensor, throttle body synchronisation, idle mixture and CO percentage. Unless you have a good knowledge of the electronic injection system and some equipment (Mathesis Tester, computer interface and software, or multimeter and probe) this is best left to a dealer.

Check that the oil pressure light doesn't come on. The oil pressure light coming on can be caused by low oil volume, or more rarely by a faulty oil pressure sensor or faulty oil pump. Whatever, the reason, if the light comes on park the bike and walk away. Riding a Ducati with an oil pressure light on is like playing Russian roulette.

If there is some hesitation during starting and the battery tests okay, it's possible the starter sprag is the culprit. Over time the sprag spring can stretch, causing a hesitation before starting. If the sprag springs stretch to the point where they slip against the starter gear the engine won't turn over. Replacing the sprag is quite involved, and requires removal of the alternator and flywheel. Sometimes the springs can be tightened by trimming, but it may be easier to replace the bearing. The sprag bearing is the same as that used on some models of BMW, KTM and Aprilia. After the engine is running, check that the gear selection isn't clunky, and that neutral is easily located. If the low charge light comes on there could be a problem with the voltage regulator or a stator malfunction.

Engine – smoke/noise

Compared to ultra-quiet modern Japanese bikes the Desmodue is mechanically quite noisy, but it shouldn't sound excessive. When the engine is running listen for a deep rumble under the alternator cover. Particularly on pre-2001 models the

4   3   2   1

alternator nut can come loose. If this happens the rotor can loosen, splitting in half and damaging the keyway and crank.

On the 907, ST2 and ST3 the cooling system can be neglected, so ask the owner when it was last serviced. Coolant should be changed every two years and hoses every five years. Although water pumps are generally reliable, thermostats can fail. Coolant reservoir tanks also have a tendency to crack, so check for signs of coolant leakage around the headstock. Any

Blip the throttle and watch for blue smoke.

coolant evident at the rear of the engine could indicate rear head gasket leakage.

Once the engine has reached operating temperature there shouldn't be any blue smoke emanating from the exhaust. Poor oil consumption and blue smoke are a sign of cylinder bore and valve guide wear, but this is generally not a problem with these engines. More likely a smoking engine may indicate the need for new piston rings. Check for oil leaks, especially around the cylinder base gasket.

Brakes

As the Desmodue range spans more than three decades there's considerable variation in brake specification. But as these bikes are not too heavy, even early bikes with small discs and twin piston calipers stop well enough. Brakes improved during the 1980s with the introduction of four-piston calipers, and the latest generation brakes are exceptional. Generally, the traditional Brembo four-piston caliper and non-radial master cylinder assembly of most of these bikes is more than adequate for street use. Whether you're looking at a Pantah with small 05 Brembo brake calipers, or a modern Monster with radial Brembo calipers, all should operate without a spongy feeling, and without pads sticking.

If the brakes are not working as well as they should it's possible the pads and discs are glazed. Scoring on the rotors indicates worn-out pads. Some pre-2001 Desmoquattros may have rubber brake lines, so check these for cracks and bulging when the brakes are applied. The standard Brembo master

Early Pantahs had small brake calipers and solid discs.

Most Desmodues have four-piston Brembo front brake calipers. These earlier 320mm steel discs were prone to warping.

cylinders aren't brilliant, and replacement with a Nissin or later radial Brembo is a sign of a conscientious owner.

Check the discs/rotors for warping and cracks. The stock steel rotors can warp after extreme use, such as on a racetrack or fast twisty road, and a rainbow pattern across the rotor indicates warping. Front-end shudder during light braking is another sign of warped rotors. All brakes need to be checked for sticking pads. If the bike doesn't roll freely as you push it, the calipers may need a strip and overhaul.

Some later versions have radial front brake calipers.

Exhaust

A rotten exhaust, whether it is header pipes or silencers that need replacing, is a major expense. Many Desmodues will have aftermarket exhaust systems, either full or slip-on, and on fuel-injected models these must be accompanied by a suitable computer chip or a Dynojet Power Commander that allows for mapping changes via a computer USB port or Palm Pilot. Carburettor versions will require modified jetting. Stock exhaust systems are generally heavier and uglier than aftermarket, and replacement carbon-fibre cans are not as durable as aluminium or stainless steel. Blip the throttle and listen for loose or rotten internals. Finally, check the oxygen sensor plugs in the exhaust pipes, as they have a tendency to fall out.

Termignoni carbon-fibre silencers are the most popular exhaust modification, but don't fit as well as some other aftermarket types.

Short Conti-style silencers won't detract from the value of a good Pantah.

Test ride

However carefully you examine the bike and listen to the engine, there's no substitute for a test ride to get a real feel for the condition it's in. This should not be less than 15 minutes, and you should be doing the riding – not the seller with you on the pillion. It's understandable that some sellers are reluctant to let a complete stranger loose on their pride and joy, but it does go with the territory of selling a bike.

As long as you leave an article of faith, usually the vehicle you arrived in, and take your driving licence everyone should be happy.

Before undertaking a test ride see if the owner allows the engine to warm up sufficiently prior to being ridden. Riding off on a cold engine is a sign of an unsympathetic owner and can lead to premature rocker wear.

The bike should start promptly, gear selection should be positive and not clunky, and clutch take-up should be smooth and progressive. Any jerkiness on take-off could indicate a worn clutch. Except for the smaller capacity (400 and 500cc) versions the Desmodue engine makes good power everywhere, so the bike should accelerate briskly in all gears, and should respond instantly, with no hiccups or hesitation. While accelerating, check that the clutch isn't slipping.

The handling on all Desmodues is excellent, but be aware that poor suspension setup can detrimentally affect the handling. Towards the end of the test ride think beyond the style and condition as to whether you would be happy owning and riding one of these. Does it fit you? Most Ducatis don't really suit very tall riders, and some sporting models, particularly the newer SportClassics, have a punishing riding position for city and urban riding.

Back at base check the engine settles into a nice steady idle before switching off. If all is well, talk to the owner about price. If you've discovered a fault and he/she won't make a deal, then thank the owner for their time and walk away. There is always another bike available somewhere.

Evaluation procedure
Add up the total points –

Score: 96 = excellent; 72 = good; 48 = average; 24 = poor. Bikes scoring over 67 will be completely usable and will require only maintenance and care to preserve condition. Bikes scoring between 24 and 49 will require some serious work (at much the same cost regardless of score). Bikes scoring between 50 and 66 will require very careful assessment of the necessary repair/restoration costs in order to arrive at a realistic value.

10 Auctions
– sold! Another way to buy your dream

Auction pros & cons

Pros: Prices will usually be lower than those of dealers or private sellers, and you might grab a real bargain on the day. Auctioneers have usually established clear title with the seller. At the venue you can usually examine documentation relating to the vehicle.

Cons: You have to rely on a sketchy catalogue description of condition and history. The opportunity to inspect is limited, and you cannot ride the bike. Auction bikes are often a little below par and may require some work. It's easy to overbid. There will usually be a buyer's premium to pay in addition to the auction hammer price.

Which auction?

Auctions by established auctioneers are advertised in bike magazines and on the auction houses' websites. A catalogue, or a simple printed list of the lots for auction, might only be available a day or two ahead, though often lots are listed and pictured on auctioneers' websites much earlier. Contact the auction company to ask if previous auction selling prices are available as this is useful information (details of past sales are often available on websites).

Catalogue, entry fee, and payment details

When you purchase the catalogue of the vehicles in the auction, it often acts as a ticket allowing two people to attend the viewing days and the auction. Catalogue details tend to be comparatively brief, but will include information such as 'one owner from new, low mileage, full service history,' etc. It will also usually show a guide price to give you some idea of what to expect to pay, and will tell you what is charged as a 'Buyer's premium.' The catalogue will also contain details of acceptable forms of payment. At the fall of the hammer an immediate deposit is usually required, the balance payable within 24 hours. If you plan to pay by cash note that there may be a cash limit. Some auctions will accept payment by debit card; and sometimes credit or charge cards are acceptable, but will often incur an extra charge. A bank draft or bank transfer will have to be arranged in advance with your own bank as well as with the auction house. No bike will be released before all payments are cleared. If delays occur in payment transfers then storage costs can accrue.

Buyer's premium

A buyer's premium will be added to the hammer price: don't forget this in your calculations. It is not usual for there to be a further state tax or local tax on the purchase price and/or on the buyer's premium.

Viewing

In some instances it's possible to view on the day, or days, before, as well as in the hours prior to the auction. There are auction officials who may be willing to help out, too, but while the officials may start the engine for you, a test ride is out of the question. Crawling under and around the bike as much as you want is permitted. You can also ask to see any documentation available.

Bidding

Before you take part in the auction, decide on your maximum bid – and stick to it!

It may take a while for the auctioneer to reach the lot you're interested in, so use that time to observe how other bidders behave. When it's the turn of your bike, attract the auctioneer's attention and make an early bid. The auctioneer will then look to you for a reaction every time another bid is made; usually the bids will be in fixed increments until the bidding slows, whereupon smaller increments will often be accepted before the hammer falls. If you want to withdraw from the bidding, make sure the auctioneer understands your intentions – a vigorous shake of the head when he or she looks to you for the next bid should do the trick!

Assuming that you are the successful bidder, the auctioneer will note your card or paddle number, and from that moment on you will be responsible for the vehicle.

If the bike is unsold, either because it failed to reach the reserve or because there was little interest, it may be possible to negotiate with the owner, via the auctioneer, after the sale is over.

Successful bid

There are two more items to think about: how to get the bike home; and insurance. If you can't ride the bike, your own or a hired trailer is one way, another is to have the vehicle shipped using the facilities of a local company. The auction house will also have details of companies specialising in the transfer of bikes.

Insurance for immediate cover can usually be purchased on site, but it may be more cost-effective to make arrangements with your own insurance company in advance, and then call to confirm the full details.

eBay & other online auctions

eBay and other online auctions could land you a bike at a bargain price, though you'd be foolhardy to bid without examining the bike first, something most vendors encourage. A useful feature of eBay is that the geographical location of the bike is shown, so you can narrow your choices to those within a realistic radius of home. Be prepared to be outbid in the last few moments of the auction. Remember, your bid is binding, and it will be very, very difficult to get restitution in the case of a crooked vendor fleecing you – caveat emptor!

Be aware that some bikes offered for sale in online auctions are 'ghost' bikes. Don't part with any cash without being sure that the vehicle does actually exist and is as described (usually pre-bidding inspection is possible).

Auctioneers

Barons www.barons.co.uk
Barrett-Jackson www.barrett-jackson.com
Bonhams www.bonhams.com
British Car Auctions (BCA)
www.bca-europe.com or
www.british-car-auctions.co.uk
Cheffins www.cheffins.co.uk
Christies www.christies.com

Coys www.coys.co.uk
Dorset Vintage and Classic Auctions
www.dvca.co.uk
eBay www.eBay.com
H&H www.classic-auctions.co.uk
RM Auctions www.rmauctions.com
Shannons www.shannons.com.au
Silver www.silverauctions.com

11 Paperwork
– correct documentation is essential

The paper trail
Pre-owned bikes come with a large portfolio of paperwork accumulated and passed on by a succession of proud owners. This documentation represents the real history of the bike, and from it can be deduced the level of care the bike has received, how much it's been used, which specialists have worked on it, and the dates of major repairs and restorations. All of this information will be priceless to you as the new owner, so be very wary of bikes with little or no paperwork to support their claimed history.

Registration documents
All countries/states have some form of registration for private vehicles, whether it's like the American 'pink slip' system or the British 'log book' systems.

It's essential to check that the registration document is genuine, that it relates to the bike in question, and that all the vehicle's details are correctly recorded, including frame and engine numbers (if these are shown). If you are buying from the previous owner, his or her name and address will be recorded in the document: this will not be the case if you're buying from a dealer.

In the UK, the current (Euro-aligned) registration document is named 'V5C,' and is printed in coloured sections of blue, green and pink. The blue section relates to the motorcycle specification, the green section has details of the new owner, and the pink section is sent to the DVLA in the UK when the bike is sold. A small section in yellow deals with selling the bike within the motor trade.

In the UK the DVLA will provide details of earlier keepers of the bike upon payment of a small fee, and much can be learned in this way.

If the bike has a foreign registration there may be expensive and time-consuming formalities to complete. Do you really want the hassle? For European buyers, importing from the USA, for example, might seem tempting, but you'll have to buy the bike sight unseen, and the paperwork to import and re-register is a daunting prospect. That means employing a shipping agent; you'll also have to budget in the shipping costs. Then there's (at the time of writing) 6% import duty on the bike and shipping costs, then 20% VAT on the whole lot. Unless you're after a rare US-only spec bike, it's not worth the hassle.

Roadworthiness certificate
Most country/state administrations require that vehicles are regularly tested to prove they are safe to use on the public highway. In the UK that test (the 'MoT') is carried out at approved testing stations, for a fee. Across the USA the requirement varies, but most states insist on an emissions test every two years as a minimum, while the police are charged with pulling over unsafe-looking vehicles.

In the UK the test is required on an annual basis once a vehicle becomes three years old. Of particular relevance for older bikes is that the certificate issued includes the mileage reading recorded at the test date and, therefore, becomes an independent record of that bike's history. Ask the seller if previous certificates are available. Without an MoT the vehicle should be taken on a flat-bed to its new home, unless you insist that a valid MoT is part of the deal. (Not such a bad idea this – at least you'll know the bike was roadworthy on the day it was tested, and you don't need to wait for the old certificate to expire before having the test done.)

Road licence

The administration of every country/state charges some kind of tax for the use of its roads; the actual form of the 'road licence' and how it's displayed, varies enormously from country-to-country and state-to-state.

Whatever the form, the road licence must relate to the vehicle carrying it, and must be present and valid if the bike is to be driven on the public highway legally. The value of the licence will depend on the length of time it's valid for.

In the UK, if a bike is untaxed because it has not been used for a period of time, the owner must inform the licensing authorities, otherwise the vehicle's date-related registration number will be lost, and there will be a painful amount of paperwork to get it re-registered.

Service history

This is a valuable record, and the more of it there is, the better. The ultimate consists of every single routine service bill (from official dealers, or known and respected independents), plus bills for all other repairs and accessories.

But really, anything helps in the great authenticity game – items like the original bill of sale, handbook, parts invoices and repair bills, all add to the story and character of the machine. Even a brochure correct to the year of the bike's manufacture is a useful document, and something that you could well have to search hard to locate in future years. If the seller claims that the bike has been restored, then expect receipts and other evidence from a specialist restorer.

If the bike has a patchy or non-existent service history, then it could still be perfectly good, but the lack of history should be reflected in the price. Many owners are competent mechanics and look after the bike themselves.

Restoration photographs

If the seller says the bike has been restored, then expect to be shown a series of photographs taken during the restoration. Pictures taken at various stages and angles, should help you gauge the thoroughness of the work. If you buy the bike, ask if you can have all the photographs, as they form an important part of its history. Many sellers are happy to part with their bike and accept your cash, but want to hang on to their photographs! If so, you may be able to persuade the vendor to get a set of copies made.

12 What's it worth?
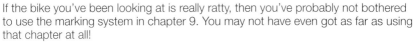
– let your head rule your heart

Condition

If the bike you've been looking at is really ratty, then you've probably not bothered to use the marking system in chapter 9. You may not have even got as far as using that chapter at all!

If you did use the marking system in chapter 9 you'll know whether the bike is in Excellent (maybe concours), Good, Average or Poor condition or, perhaps, somewhere in-between these categories.

To keep up-to-date with prices, buy the latest editions of bike magazines (also *Bike Trader* and *MCN* in the UK) and check the classified and dealer ads – these are particularly useful as they let you compare private and dealer prices. Most of the dealers will have up-to-date websites as well. It is also useful to check eBay prices, as this is generally a good guide to market value.

Desmodue Ducatis are relatively modern machines, and, as production covers more than thirty years, there are a lot of them around. Some will undoubtedly be considered classics in the future, and these will be the rarer limited edition F1s and possibly the more recent MH900e and Paul Smart 1000. Pantahs and early Monsters and Supersports will always be the cheapest, but prices are probably about as low as they will go.

Depreciation will affect all newer examples, but as most of these bikes have now been superseded this is less likely to be a problem. Before you start haggling with the seller, consider what effect any variation from standard specification might have on the bike's value. Originality is not really an issue except for the more collectable models, and many owners, particularly of Monsters, fit expensive aftermarket exhaust systems, brakes, and engine upgrades. Most of these aftermarket additions will increase the bike's value, but not to the extent of the outlay involved, and it may work in your favour. If you're buying from a dealer, remember there will be a dealer's premium on the price.

Striking a deal

Negotiate on the basis of your condition assessment, mileage, and fault rectification cost. Also take into account the bike's specification. Be realistic about the value, but don't be completely intractable: a small compromise on the part of the vendor or buyer will often facilitate a deal at little real cost.

13 Do you really want to restore?
– it'll take longer and cost more than you think

There's a romance about restoration projects, about bringing a sick bike back to its original glory. It's tempting to buy something that needs a few things to bring it up to scratch,but there are several things to consider. Once you've got the bike home and start taking it apart, a few small jobs can soon become large ones. Restoration is also extremely expensive and time-consuming. Will you get as much pleasure from working on the bike as you will riding it?

This applies to restoring any bike, but in the case of a Desmodue Ducati, you need to think long and hard. Most of these bikes are too numerous, and not collectable enough, to be considered an investment. There's no doubt some Desmodues can be considered classics, but apart from a few select models this hasn't translated into appreciating values just yet. So, if you do buy a cheap and tacky bike, its increased value as a result of your restoration is unlikely to justify the time and money spent. That said, the benefits of restoration should not be overlooked, in particular the feeling of accomplishment in knowing you have removed and installed every component on the motorcycle. During a restoration, design flaws can be corrected and appropriate modifications made, and a well-restored bike can be superior to the condition it was in when it left the factory.

Restoring a Desmodue yourself requires a number of skills, which is fine if you already have them, but if you haven't it's good not to make your newly acquired bike part of the learning curve. Are you confident about building an engine, and do you have a sufficient range of tools? Restorations test the limits of a tool chest, and it's important to be organised when a bike is disassembled. Depending on the condition of the bike you must also be prepared to spend a lot of time on the restoration process.

A rolling restoration is tempting, especially as the summers start to pass and your bike's off the road. Unfortunately, subjecting the bike to road grime while restoring is not the way to achieve a concours finish. A concours finish requires a complete strip down and nut-and-bolt rebuild, but a rolling restoration has its merits. Riding helps you maintain an interest as the bike's condition improves, and doing things gradually can spread the cost. In the long run it will take longer, but you'll get some on-road fun in the meantime.

This well-used bike may not be 100% original but has been carefully maintained and will still be a good buy.

14 Paint problems
– bad complexion, including dimples, pimples and bubbles

Paint faults generally occur due to a lack of protection/maintenance, or to poor preparation prior to a respray or touch-up. Some of the following conditions may be present in the bike you're looking at:

Orange peel
This appears as an uneven paint surface, similar to the appearance of the skin of an orange. The fault is caused by the failure of atomised paint droplets to flow into each other when they hit the surface. It's sometimes possible to rub out the effect with proprietary paint cutting/rubbing compound or very fine grades of abrasive paper. A respray may be may be necessary in severe cases. Consult a paint shop for advice.

Cracking
Severe cases are likely to have been caused by too heavy an application of paint (or filler beneath the paint). Also, insufficient stirring of the paint before application can lead to the components being improperly mixed, and cracking can result. Incompatibility with the paint already on the panel can have a similar effect. To rectify the problem it is necessary to rub down to a smooth, sound finish before respraying the problem area.

Crazing
Sometimes the paint takes on a crazed rather than a cracked appearance when the problems mentioned under 'Cracking' are present. This problem can also be caused by a reaction between the underlying surface and the paint. Paint removal and respraying the problem area is usually the only solution.

Blistering
Almost always caused by corrosion of the metal beneath the paint. Usually perforation will be found in the metal and the damage will usually be worse than that suggested by the area of blistering. The metal will have to be repaired before repainting.

Micro blistering
Usually the result of an economy respray where inadequate heating has allowed moisture to settle on the car before spraying. Consult a paint specialist, but usually damaged paint will have to be removed before partial or full respraying. Can also be caused by bike covers that don't 'breathe.'

Fading
Some colours, especially reds, are prone to fading if subjected to strong sunlight for long periods without the benefit of polish protection. Sometimes proprietary paint restorers and/or paint cutting/rubbing compounds will remedy the situation, but often a respray is the only real solution.

Peeling
Often a problem with metallic paintwork when the sealing lacquer becomes

damaged and begins to peel off. Poorly applied paint may also peel. The remedy is to strip and start again!

Dimples
Dimples in the paintwork are caused by the residue of polish (particularly silicone types) not being removed properly before respraying. Paint removal and repainting is the only solution.

Check the bodywork for damage. This can be a particular problem with early fibreglass seats like this 750 F1.

This bodywork damage is more serious.

15 Problems due to lack of use

– just like their owners, Desmodues need exercise!

Like any piece of engineering, Desmodue Ducatis deteriorate if they sit doing nothing for long periods. It's better to buy a properly maintained, higher mileage bike as these motorcycles can suffer all sorts of problems if left sitting with bad fuel. Fuel filters clog, fuel lines deteriorate, coolant leaks can occur, and batteries go bad, all of which means a lot of work for a prospective new owner.

Rust

If a bike is put away wet and/or stored in a damp garage, the paint, metal and brightwork will suffer. Ensure the machine is completely dry and clean before going into storage. Invest in a dehumidifier to keep the garage atmosphere dry. Exhaust gas has a high water content, so exhaust systems corrode very quickly from the inside when the bike is not used. Steel fuel tanks can rust and filters clog if stale fuel is left in for a long period.

Seized components

Brake fluid absorbs water from the atmosphere, and should be renewed every two years. Old fluid with a high water content can cause corrosion and pistons/calipers to seize (freeze), and can cause brake failure when the water turns to vapour near hot braking components. Cables are vulnerable to seizure, too. They should be thoroughly lubed before the bike is put in storage, and the levers pulled regularly.

Tyres

If the bike has been left on its side stand, most of its weight is on the tyres, causing cracks and flat spots. Always leave the bike on the centre-stand, as this will take some weight off the tyres. If there's no centre stand

Check wheels for corrosion.

Brake calipers can seize.

move the bike a foot or so once a week. A paddock stand will keep the rear wheel off the ground.

Engine
Old, acidic, oil can corrode bearings. Many riders change the oil in the spring, when they're putting the bike back on the road, but really it should be changed just before the bike is laid up, so the bearings are sitting in fresh oil. When you're giving the cables their weekly exercise don't start the engine. Running the engine for a short time will do more harm than good, as it produces a lot of internal moisture which won't burn off as the engine doesn't get hot enough. This moisture will attack the engine internals and silencers.

Battery/electrics
Remove the battery and give it a top up charge every couple of weeks, or connect it to a battery top-up device, such as the Optimate, which will keep it permanently fully charged. Damp conditions will cause fuses and earth connections to corrode, creating potential electrical troubles come spring. Wiring insulation can also harden and fail.

16 The Community

– key people, organisations and companies in the Ducati world

Auctioneers
See Chapter 10

Useful websites and clubs across the world
Ducati Owners' club GB
http://www.docgb.org/
Desmo Owners' club
http://www.ducati.com/club/index.do
US Desmo Club
http://www.usdesmo.com/
Ducati Owners' club New Zealand
http://www.docnz.co.nz/
Ducati Owners' club NSW
http://www.docnsw.org.au/
Ducati Owners' club Victoria
http://www.docv.org/
Canberra District Ducati Club
http://www.cddc.org.au/
Ducati Club WA
http://www.docwa.com.au/
Ducati Club Queensland
http://www.docq.com.au/
Ducati Club France
http://www.desmo-net.com/
Ducati Pompone Italia
http://www.pompone.com/
Ducati Club Netherlands
http://www.ducaticlub.nl/
Ducati Club Sweden
http://www.ducatiklubben.se/
Ducati Club Denmark
http://www.ducati.dk/
Ducati Club Munich
http://www.ducati-club-muenchen.de/
Ducati Club Austria
http://www.ducatimc.at/

Specialists (UK)
There are many specialists so this list is more representative than comprehensive. This list does not imply recommendation.

Sigma Performance
http://www.sigmaperformance.com/
Neil Spalding's excellent specialist workshop in Tunbridge Wells, Kent Ph 01892 538802 or 0788 1820 748

MotoRapido
http://www.motorapido.co.uk/
Specialist workshop in Winchester, Hampshire

Ducati John
http://www.ducati-john.co.uk/
Specialist servicing by John Cellier at Rothwell, West Yorkshire

GTEC Performance
http://www.gtecperformance.co.uk/
Jeff Green's specialist workshop Ph 01858 535 411 or 0784 1099 998

MD Racing
http://www.md-racing.co.uk/
Mike Dawson 07783 024 248 Walton on Thames, Surrey

Books
Ducati Belt-Drive Two-Valve Twins Restoration Guide
Ian Falloon, Octane Press 2012
The Ducati Story 5th Edition
Ian Falloon, Haynes, 2011
Standard Catalog of Ducati Motorcycles 1946-2005
Ian Falloon, Kraus Publications, 2006
The Ducati 750 Bible Ian Falloon, Veloce
The Ducati 860, 900 and Mille Bible Ian Falloon, Veloce

– essential data at your fingertips

We can't list details of every Desmodue variant here so have picked three representative bikes: 1981 500 SL Pantah; 1994 900 Monster; and 2007 Hypermotard.

Engine

1981 500 SL Pantah: Air-cooled, 90-degree two-valve v-twin, 499cc. Bore and stroke 74x58mm, compression ratio 9.5:1, 45bhp at 9050rpm
1994 900 Monster: Air-cooled, 90-degree two-valve v-twin, 904cc. Bore and stroke 92x68mm, compression ratio 9.2:1, 80bhp at 7250rpm
2007 1100 Hypermotard: Air-cooled, 90-degree two-valve v-twin, 1079cc. Bore and stroke 98x71.5mm, compression ratio 10.5:1, 90bhp at 7750rpm

Gearbox

1981 500 SL Pantah: Five-speed. Ratios: 1st 1:0.400; 2nd 1:0.583; 3rd 1:0.750; 4th 1:0.931; 5th 1:1.074
1994 900 Monster: Six-speed. Ratios: 1st 1:0.405; 2nd 1:0.566; 3rd 1:0.741; 4th 1:0.916; 5th 1:1.043; 6th 1:1.166
2007 1100 Hypermotard: Six-speed. Ratios: 1st 1:0.405; 2nd 1:0.566; 3rd 1:0.741; 4th 1:0.916; 5th 1:1.043; 6th 1:1.166

Brakes

1981 500 SL Pantah: Front 2x 260mm discs, twin-piston calipers, rear 260mm disc, twin-piston caliper
1994 900 Monster: Front 2x 320mm discs, four-piston calipers, rear 245mm disc, twin-piston caliper
2007 1100 Hypermotard: Front 2x 305mm discs, four-piston calipers, rear 245mm disc, twin-piston caliper

Electrics

1981 500 SL Pantah: 12-volt, 200W alternator
1994 900 Monster: 12-volt, 350W alternator
2007 1100 Hypermotard: 12-volt, alternator Marelli EFI

Weight (dry)

1981 500 SL Pantah: 180kg
1994 900 Monster: 185kg
2007 1100 Hypermotard: 179kg

Max speed

1981 500 SL Pantah: 122mph
1994 900 Monster: 124mph+
2007 1100 Hypermotard: 125mph+

Major change points by model years

1979 500 SL Pantah enters limited production
1981 600 SL Pantah production commences

1982 350 XL, 600 TL introduced

1983 350 and 650 SL Pantah released. 600 SL available in MHR colours

1985 Cagiva Alazzurra and 750 F1 introduced

1986 750 F1 updated, accompanied by Indiana cruiser, 350 and 400 F3 and limited edition Montjuich. 750 Paso heralds a new era for Ducati

1987 Limited edition 750 F1 Laguna Seca introduced

1988 906 Paso replaces the 750, and the final limited edition 750 F1, the Santamonica released. Nuovo 750 Sport appears

1989 Only new series Pantah engines now in production, Weber carburettor 900 SS joining the 750 Sport and 906 Paso

1990 No changes and the only new model the 400 SS for Japan

1991 New 900, 750 and 400 Supersports, alongside 907ie

1992 Only minor updates to existing models this year. First series 900 SL introduced

1993 First year for the 900 Monster

1994 600 Supersport and 600 Monster introduced. 750 Supersport receives a dual disc front brake

1995 Cosmetic changes to the Supersport and Monster line-ups. Gold frame colour as for 916

1996 750 Monster introduced. 900 Monster received an adjustable front fork

1997 Supersports received new graphics. 900 Monster with small valve lower output engine. ST2 released

1998 Higher spec 900 S Monster and 900 Cromo introduced. Silver 900 SS Final Edition and new fuel-injected 900 Supersport released

1999 New 750 Supersport joins 900. Monster range now includes the Dark and City

2000 900 Monster is restyled and receives fuel-injection

2001 Limited edition MH900e and entry level 750 Sport introduced

2002 1000 DS Multistrada released. 620 ie Monster replaces the 600 and 750 ie Monster and 900 Sport introduced

2003 Supersport and Monster ranges updated to include three capacities: 620, 800 and 1000

2004 Three-valve ST3 replaces ST2. New six-speed 620 Monster released

2005 S2R Monster introduced and Multistrada updated

2006 Final year for the 1000DS Supersport. SportClassic range, ST3S with ABS, and 1000S2R introduced. Monster 695 replaces 620

2007 Hypermotard 1100 and 1100S released. Multistrada also receives 1100cc engine. Sport 1000 and GT 1000 now the only SportClassics available

2008 New generation Monster 696 replaces 695

2009 Monster 1100 and 1100S introduced. Final year for Desmodue Multistrada

2010 Only SportClassic the GT1000. 796 and higher specification 1100 EVO Hypermotard released. Final year for the GT 1000 SportClassic

2011 New 1100 EVO and 796 Monster

2012 Monster 1100 Diesel and Hypermotard 1100 EVO SP Corse Edition introduced

2013 Monster 1100, 796, and 696 only remaining air-cooled two-valve twins

Engine number/frame number/VIN

Engine and frame numbers do not match, and each model often used a different number series. Vehicle identification is by a 17-digit VIN on the steering head. This varies from country to country, and can be checked here: http://www.motoverse.com/tools/vin/ducati.asp

The Essential Buyer's Guide™ series ...

978-1-845840-22-8

978-1-845840-26-6

978-1-845840-29-7

978-1-845840-77-8

978-1-845840-99-0

978-1-904788-70-6

978-1-845841-01-0

978-1-845841-19-5

978-1-845841-13-3

978-1-845841-35-5

978-1-845841-36-2

978-1-845841-38-6

978-1-845841-46-1

978-1-845841-47-8

978-1-845841-63-8

978-1-845841-65-2

978-1-845841-88-1

978-1-845841-92-8

978-1-845842-00-0

978-1-845842-04-8

978-1-845842-05-5

978-1-845842-70-3

978-1-845842-81-9

978-1-845842-83-3

978-1-845842-84-0

978-1-845842-87-1

978-1-84584-134-8

978-1-845843-03-8

978-1-845843-09-0

978-1-845843-16-8

978-1-845843-29-8

978-1-845843-30-4

978-1-845843-34-2

978-1-845843-38-0

978-1-845843-39-7

978-1-845841-61-4

978-1-845842-31-4

978-1-845843-07-6

978-1-845843-40-3

978-1-845843-48-9

978-1-845843-63-2
978-1-845844-09-7

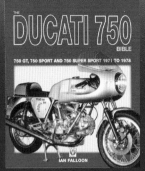

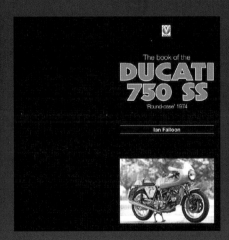

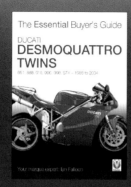
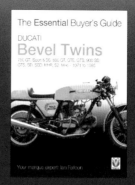
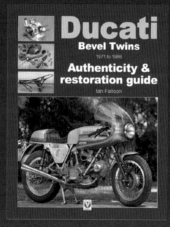

Index